15 WAYS TO SUCCESSFULLY MARKET YOUR CHILD CARE BUSINESS

By

TIMEKA WILLIAMS

Copyright © 2016

ACKNOWLEDGEMENTS

I'd like to thank my son Tideverett Harper! I love you and I'm thankful that you support me in all my dreams!

Thanks Shana Isaac for the continuous phone conversations about child care and improving our businesses.

Thanks Randolph Mapp, Jr. for believing in my vision.

ABOUT THE AUTHOR

Timeka Williams is CEO of Bookkeeper Lady, a leading Tax Preparation, Bookkeeping, Payroll Processing and Business Consulting agency in the Atlanta Metro area. Her marketing work has included successful consultation and campaigns for many companies. She also owns Attentive Safety CPR and Safety Training, which conducts CPR and Safety classes all over the United States. Timeka is a featured speaker for numerous companies and seminars as well as a guest lecturer for universities. She has also been the CEO of Primary Kids Childcare and Early Foundations Learning Center. You can follow her on Twitter at http://twitter.com/timekawilliams.

INTRODUCTION

With so many children being born each day, you'd think it would be all too easy to have your child care program to full capacity each week. But it can be tough. Meeting new people means putting you and your business out there and risking rejection, and simply most of us would rather avoid this. However you've worked hard to build your business and the last thing you'd want to do is fail due to lack of knowledge or fear of rejection.

In this book, I'll show you 15 realistic and profitable ways to market your child care business. If you market your business correctly, there's no limit to what you can accomplish!

Table of Contents

ACKNOWLEDGEMENTS

ABOUT THE AUTHOR

Introduction

I. ....Get Online

    1. Twitter

    Understand the Basic Concept of Twitter

    Your Twitter Profile

    Be an Active Tweeter

2. ....Facebook

    Understand the Basic Concept of Facebook

    Your Facebook Profile

    Stay Active on Facebook

3. ....LinkedIn

    Understand the Basic Concept of LinkedIn

    Your LinkedIn Profile

    Stay Active on LinkedIn

4. ....Blogging

    Start Your Own Blog

    Update Your Blog Consistently

5. ....E-mail Signature

6. ....Craigslist

    Understand the Basic Concept of Craigslist

    Post Regularly On Craigslist

7. ....Instagram

      Understand the Basic Concept of Instagram

      Your Instagram Profile

      Post Regularly On Instagram

II. ....Get Up, Get Out and Meet People

8. .....Start With People Whom You've Lost Touch With

9. ....Area Schools

10. ....Business Cards

11. ....Corporate Discounts

12. ....Dress the Part

13. ....Advertising Pens

14. ....Advertising Coloring Pages and Crayons

15. ....Seek Out Public Speaking Opportunities

III. ....Summary

I. GET ONLINE

1. TWITTER

UNDERSTAND THE BASIC CONCEPT OF TWITTER

Twitter is an online communication tool that people use for various reasons whether business or personal. Anything that you put on Twitter will be sent out for your network or the universe to see. It's a great platform to find people and business with similar interests as you.

YOUR TWITTER PROFILE

Make sure you have a complete profile that is attractive and compliments your business. Before people follow you, they will check out your profile on Twitter. You should have an avatar that represents your business well. Put some thought into it!

BE AN ACTIVE TWEETER

If you want to build a strong following, you'll need to post content. Mention other businesses whom you purchase merchandise from or share updates about your child care business so it attracts parents in the area. Keep your posts relevant and frequent. Also share posts from popular charitable organizations or noncompetitive businesses with relevant content about the child care industry to build your network.

2. FACEBOOK

UNDERSTAND THE BASIC CONCEPT OF FACEBOOK

Facebook is primarily setup as a place for friends to connect, share pictures and play games. However there is great networking and marketing opportunities available there.

YOUR FACEBOOK PROFILE

Create a business Facebook profile for your business. Look through all your friends and invite them to like your page. If they have used your child care services, invite them to review your business. If you don't have many Facebook friends, start now to make connections with people you know or may at least be associated with.

STAY ACTIVE ON FACEBOOK

"Like" and "Share" other businesses or people's links. Post regular content about your child care business. Comment on people's or businesses status updates.

3. LINKEDIN

UNDERSTAND THE BASIC CONCEPT OF LINKEDIN

LinkedIn is a social networking site for professionals looking for employment and also used to make business connections.

YOUR LINKEDIN PROFILE

Create a personal LinkedIn page as a Child Care professional to network with others in the industry. Create a business LinkedIn page and get your staff involved. There's a section where you can provide detailed information about your child care business as well as get reviews from others.

STAY ACTIVE ON LINKEDIN

Start connecting with people you know. Look through your connections' connections. Don't be afraid to ask for a recommendation. Join groups and take part in conversation.

4. BLOGGING

START YOUR OWN BLOG

A blog is a shortened form of we**b log**. It's simply an online journal where you can write whatever you want. Talk about your child care business and share your content with your social media audiences on Facebook, LinkedIn and Twitter.

UPDATE YOUR BLOG CONSISTENTLY

Make sure you post regularly! Parents may take interest that you even have the time to blog as a busy child care professional. Blogging shows that you take the time to reflect your ideas and are passionate about what you do.

5. E-MAIL SIGNATURE

Your digital signature is very important so don't underestimate it! It's at the bottom of every e-mail you send. Along with your name, your digital signature can include your occupation, contact information and anything else you'd like to share. For example, my own digital signature looks like this:

Timeka Williams

American Heart Association

Basic Life Support (BLS) Instructor

(877) 531-2226

info@attentivesafety.com

www.**attentivesafety**.com

6. CRAIGSLIST

UNDERSTAND THE BASIC CONCEPT OF CRAIGSLIST

Craigslist.com is the leading online source for classified ads. When parents are looking for child care this is a commonly searched community source. Make sure your posting stands out with a lot of detailed information including contact information, prices and hours of operation.

POST REGULARLY ON CRAIGSLIST

If you have child care openings be very descriptive and include that information in your post. Do not let your posts expire. Share your posting link with your social network platform like Facebook, LinkedIn and Twitter. If you are at capacity, be sure to still keep your company relevant by letting parents know when you expect to have openings or how and when to get added to your waiting list.

7. INSTAGRAM

UNDERSTAND THE BASIC CONCEPT OF INSTAGRAM

Instagram is an online mobile photo-sharing, video-sharing, and social networking service that enables its users to take pictures and videos and also share them.

YOUR INSTAGRAM PROFILE

Make sure you create an Instagram Business Profile. You have the option to link your Instagram Business Profile with your Facebook Business page. Make sure your profile represents your child care business well and is very attractive. Be sure to include your website and contact information.

POST REGULARLY ON INSTAGRAM

Use hashtags and post pictures regularly. With the Parents' permission, post pictures of children and their daily activities. Posting adorable pictures on a regular basis is a good way to build your child care business brand.

II. GET UP, GET OUT AND MEET PEOPLE

8. START WITH PEOPLE WHOM YOU'VE LOST TOUCH WITH

Now that you have your child care business it's time to let everybody know. It's easy to forget people you already know like old classmates, coworkers and connections you've already made.

Talk to your friends and family, let them know what you're trying to do so that they can help you accomplish this task. You never know what old friends might be up to these days and it may be a lot of fun getting back in touch with them.

9. AREA SCHOOLS

Local elementary schools are a great resource if you offer before school, after school or transportation services. Also teachers may be in need of your child care service since the schools you'll contact are in close proximity to you. It's important to maintain good relationships with the administrators of the local schools you contact and to also have good marketing material available so they may either distribute to parents or make it accessible for them to view. There may also be sponsorship opportunities available for you to place an advertisement in a yearbook, etc. in exchange for a donation.

10. BUSINESS CARDS

Create a memorable business card and always have a lot of them with you. Make sure you attempt to leave your business card with everyone you come in contact within your local area. It's likely that someone knows of someone who has children within the age range that you serve in your child care program or will come in contact with them. Your business cards should represent your business well and be of high quality. Your network is your net worth so be sure to ask for a business card as well.

11. CORPORATE DISCOUNTS

Contact local businesses and ask if they'd like their business to join your corporate discount program. Working parents are a large chunk of the employment sector and offering a discount on child care is a win-win for both companies. Explain how this will be an additional company benefit and will cut down on the burden or hassle of current or new employees finding quality child care. Be ready to explain the benefits and have your corporate discount program explained in a brochure to leave with Human Resources, Store Managers, Owners. Etc.

12. DRESS THE PART

You are a walking billboard for your child care business! Make sure that you are attractive at all times. If you work out a gym, wear a shirt that advertises your child care business. If you are running errands during business hours, wear your name badge, etc. Dress for success! Exude confidence! Use a firm handshake. Look people in the eye when you talk to them. Make your first impression your best impression.

13.   ADVERTISING PENS

Order pens with your child care business name, phone number and website on them. Take these pens and give them to servers at local restaurants for customers to sign their credit card receipts. Instruct the servers to allow the customer to keep the pen. Most servers have to purchase pens with their own money on a constant basis because customers either steal or lose the borrowed pens. This will bring cheer to servers knowing that you can provide them with pens and they will call on you when they are running low on pen inventory.

14. ADVERTISING COLORING PAGES AND CRAYONS

Customize a coloring page with your child care business contact information and make several copies. Take these pages along with a few crayons to local businesses like nail salons, tire shops, dentists, pediatricians, etc. Kids love to color! Their coloring sheet will be a work of art on the refrigerator doubling as an advertisement for your business. Make sure that you replenish the coloring sheets and crayons on a regular basis.

15. SEEK OUT PUBLIC SPEAKING OPPORTUNITIES

Do you want to get your child care business in front of a lot of people at one time? Be a featured speaker in front of a whole room that is listening. Join your local chamber of commerce, industry organizations, workforce development agencies, etc. Let them know that you're available and ready to speak. There will most definitely be people in the room who can utilize the services you provide or know someone who can.

III. SUMMARY

1. Visualize success

You must have a clear vision in your head of what successful child care business looks like.

2. What do you intend to give?

You get what you give! Are you delivering a quality child care service?

3. Have a definite date you want to achieve your desired success.
4. Have a definite plan of action to achieve your desired success.
5. Write your statement of desire identifying your visualized success, what you intend to give, by what date and with what plan.
6. Read this aloud twice daily!

God loves you and I love you too! Thanks for buying my book!